...002 White-Thomson Publishing Ltd

...duced for Hodder Wayland by
...ite-Thomson Publishing Ltd
... St Andrew's Place
...ves
...7 1UP

Editor: Anna Lee
Designer: Derek Lee
Picture Researcher: Shelley Noronha, Glass Onion Pictures
Science Panel Illustrator: Derek Lee
Map Illustrator: Tim Mayer
Consultant: Dr Brian Bowers, Senior Research Fellow at the Science Museum, London.

Cover and title page: Michael Faraday, The Royal Institution/Hodder Wayland Picture Library

Published in Great Britain in 2002 by Hodder Wayland, an imprint of Hodder Children's Books.

British Library Cataloguing in Publication Data
Ross, Stewart
  Michael Faraday. – (Scientists who made history)
  1. Faraday, Michael, 1791-1867 2. Physicists – Great Britain
  – Biography – Juvenile literature
  I. Title II. Lee, Anna
  530'.092

ISBN 07502 3939 5

Printed and bound in Italy by G. Canale & C.Sp.A, Turin.

Hodder Children's Books
A division of Hodder Headline Limited
338 Euston Road, London, NW1 3BH

Picture Acknowledgements: John Bethell/Bridgeman Art Library 22; Corbis 7, 17b; Mary Evans 9, 12t, 23, 30, 37; The Fine Art Society/Bridgeman Art Library 33; Hodder Wayland Picture Library 35, 36; Peter Newark 15b; Popperfoto 21, 25, 28t, 32, 43t; Science Photo Library 10, 13, 17t, 18, 19, 29, 31, 38, 40b; Science and Society Picture Library 20t, 28b; Private Collection/Bridgeman Art Library 15t, 20b, 24; Private Collection/Christie's Images/ Bridgeman Art Library 40t; The Royal Institution cover, 1, 11, 12b, 41; The Royal Institution, London, UK/Bridgeman Art Library 4, 5, 8, 14, 16, 26 27, 34, 39, 43b; White-Thomson Picture Library 42.

Michael
FARADAY

Stewart Ross

an imprint of Hodder Children's Books

Contents

1831: Continuous Current

MICHAEL FARADAY PAUSED for a moment, dipped his pen in the ink-well, then carried on making notes. He had been working for eight hours without a break, rearranging the equipment on his workbench and writing in his notebook.

Charles Anderson, Faraday's only laboratory assistant, glanced towards his master and sighed. The professor is like a man possessed, he thought. It's not good for his health – or mine!

BELOW: *Alone in his laboratory – a picture of Faraday at work in the basement of the Royal Institution. Notice the lack of electric light, which had yet to be invented.*

Anderson was a well-mannered man, an ex-Royal Artillery sergeant with a strong sense of loyalty. He also had enormous respect for the handsome, middle-aged Professor Faraday. But his patience was wearing thin.

With a loud sigh, he took out his watch. Half-past ten at night! The professor might be the cleverest man in all England, but was it fair to keep his assistant in the chilly basement of the Royal Institution until this hour?

Anderson coughed, hoping to attract Faraday's attention. Wrapped up in his work, the professor seemed not to hear. Anderson stood up and marched around the laboratory, banging his arms against his sides to keep warm. Still the professor took no notice.

Cold, hungry and frustrated, Anderson sat down and looked at his watch again. Suddenly, Faraday glanced up and exclaimed,

'Oh! Anderson! Still here? What time is it?'

'Almost eleven o'clock, sir. And I'm still here,' replied the gloomy assistant.

'I do apologize,' said Faraday sincerely. 'I'm getting nowhere now. We must try again tomorrow. Is that all right?'

'Of course sir,' nodded Anderson wearily. One by one, he began putting out the laboratory candles.

IN THEIR OWN WORDS

FARADAY'S ABILITY TO DEVOTE HIMSELF ENTIRELY TO HIS RESEARCH WAS WELL KNOWN. CHARLES WHEATSTONE, A FELLOW SCIENTIST, CALLED TO SEE HIM IN OCTOBER 1838 AND WROTE AFTERWARDS TO A FRIEND:

'I called on Faraday this morning and was told that this was one of the days on which he denies himself to everybody for the purpose of pursuing uninterruptedly his own researches. He will be visible tomorrow.'

RIGHT: *Michael Faraday aged about fifty.*

THE FIRST DYNAMO

Faraday was excited when he arrived at the laboratory the following day. He had been thinking about his experiment all day and urgently wanted to try something.

Anderson had set out the apparatus as before (see panel): a copper disc that rotated on an axle, an iron magnet with its poles projecting over the disc, and wires leading to a galvanometer, an instrument for measuring electrical current.

For two months Faraday had been exploring the relationship between electricity and magnetism. He talked of 'induction', which meant producing an electric current by magnetism. This was a complete mystery to Anderson, who had no formal scientific training. After taking off his coat, Faraday held one of the wires against the disc's axle and the other near its edge.

'Now, Anderson, please turn the disc,' he called.

The assistant gently rotated the disc.

'No, no!' cried Faraday. 'Give it a good spin!'

Anderson sent the copper wheel whirling round.

'Look!' shouted Faraday immediately. 'Look at the galvanometer, Mr Anderson!'

Glancing across at the instrument, the assistant saw that it was showing a steady current of electricity.

Faraday dropped the wires and reached for his notebook. 'That's it, Anderson,' he said with a look of quiet delight. 'We have induced a steady current.'

FARADAY'S DYNAMO

Faraday's experiments in 1831 succeeded in turning movement (between a conductor and a magnet) into electricity. His first experiments induced pulses of electricity by moving a magnet near a wire. The copper disc experiment induced a steady current across the rotating disc.

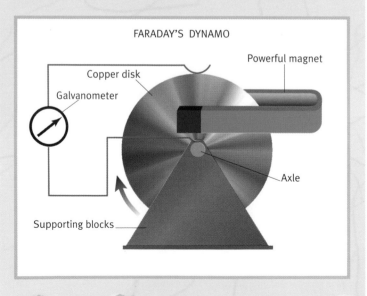

FARADAY'S DYNAMO

Copper disk
Galvanometer
Powerful magnet
Axle
Supporting blocks

Michael Faraday had invented the dynamo. This meant that mechanical energy, produced by a person, by water power or by a machine such as a steam-engine, could be turned into electricity. He was interested in scientific theory, however, not business or personal gain. Rather than developing the practical side of his ideas, he left other inventors to explore the practical applications of his discoveries. Their inventions would show that in the autumn of 1831 Michael Faraday had laid the foundations of the modern electrical industry – and changed for ever the way we live.

BELOW: *The great American inventor Thomas Edison (1847-1931, centre, in bow tie) and his laboratory staff. Many of his 1,000 inventions depended on Faraday's pioneering work.*

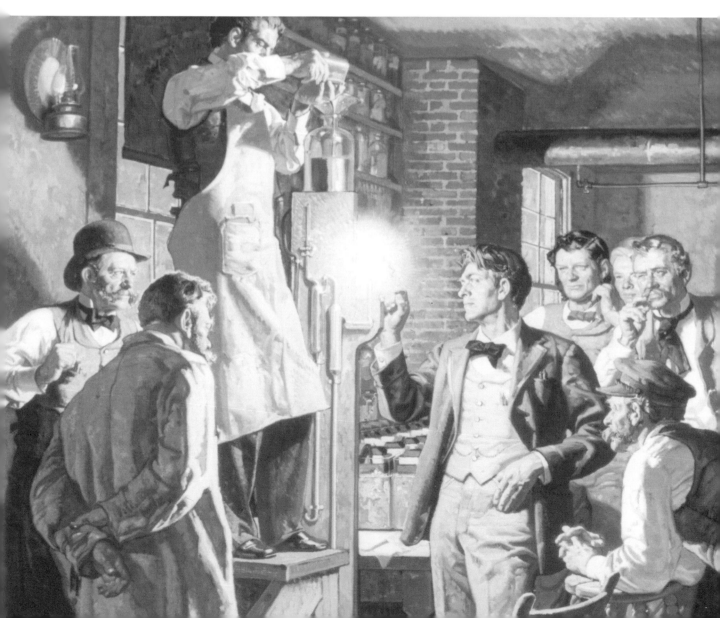

Faraday's World

MICHAEL FARADAY WAS born in Newington, Surrey, a small village that is now part of London. His birthday – 22 September 1791 – came in an age of revolutions. The war of the American Revolution had ended in 1783; the French Revolution was at its height; in Britain, the Industrial Revolution was under way.

The Industrial Revolution would change Britain into a country of industrial towns and cities. Industrial processes relied on science and technology. One day, Faraday's scientific work would have an enormous impact in this field.

Electricity

When Faraday was born, however, science was in its infancy. Electricity was still largely a mystery. Luigi Galvani (1737-98) had showed that there was electricity within animals. Later, another Italian, Alessandro Volta (1745-1827), made a second, more important breakthrough.

In 1800 Volta produced a steady electric current using plates of zinc and copper dipped in salt water. He also developed the first type of cell or battery, known as a 'Volta's pile'. This invention made possible much of Faraday's work with electricity.

BELOW: *The small house in Newington, near London, where Michael Faraday was born in 1791. The horse has been brought so that Michael's blacksmith father can replace its shoes.*

LEFT: *Alessandro Volta, the Italian scientist who put forward the theory that electricity flows in currents. He is holding his latest invention, the electric battery – then known as 'Volta's pile'.*

Chemistry

Chemistry, too, was entering a new era. The idea of four elements – earth, fire, air and water – had been replaced by Robert Boyle's (1627-91) more accurate notion. An element, he suggested, was a substance that could not be divided up.

Two scientists whose lives overlapped with Faraday's, Henry Cavendish (1731-1810) and John Dalton (1766-1844), developed chemistry further still. Cavendish discovered hydrogen and realized water could be broken down into two substances, hydrogen and oxygen. Dalton came up with an atomic theory: all matter was made up of indivisible atoms.

IN THEIR OWN WORDS

IN A LETTER TO A FRIEND, BENJAMIN ABBOTT, FARADAY DESCRIBED HOW HE MADE HIS OWN 'VOLTA'S PILE' (BATTERY):

'I, Sir, I my own self, cut out seven discs [of zinc] the size of halfpennies each. I, Sir, covered them with seven halfpences and interposed them between seven or six pieces of paper soaked in a solution of muriate of soda.'

The Young Genius

THE FARADAYS WERE not well off. James Faraday, Michael's blacksmith father, was often ill and short of work. Later, Faraday remembered living for a whole week on one loaf of bread.

As was usual then, the Faradays' cramped rented rooms had no running water or flushing toilet. The only lighting was simple oil lamps. The family took strength from the quiet courage of Michael's mother Margaret, a woman of great wisdom, and their Sandemanian religion (see panel).

A basic education

After Michael's birth, the Faradays moved to London, where James hoped to find more work. Here their last child, Margaret, was born in 1802. Michael enjoyed the company of Elizabeth and Robert, his older brother and sister, but little Margaret was always his favourite.

BELOW: *First job – the bookshop in London where Faraday worked as an apprentice bookbinder after finishing his basic schooling.*

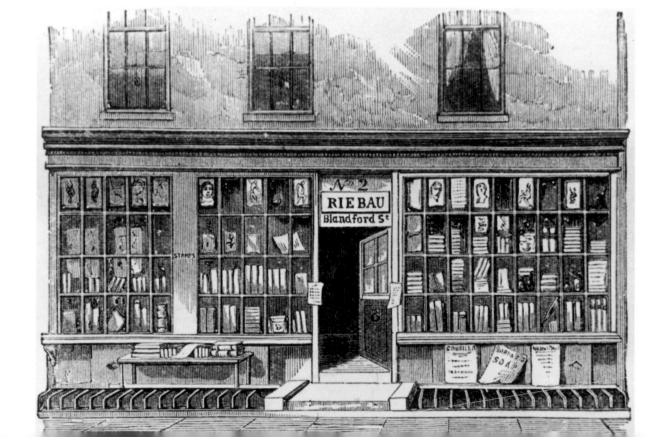

IN THEIR OWN WORDS

THE SANDEMANIANS WERE A PROTESTANT SECT THAT BELIEVED EVERY WORD OF THE BIBLE AND TRIED TO LIVE LIKE THE FIRST CHRISTIANS. THEY CHOSE THEIR OWN LEADERS, REJECTED FAME AND RICHES, AND SAID ALL PEOPLE WERE EQUAL. FARADAY ACCEPTED SANDEMANIAN TEACHING WITHOUT QUESTION. ONE SANDEMANIAN REMEMBERED FARADAY SHARING HIS FAITH WITH VERY ORDINARY WORKING MEN:

'Michael Faraday was one of the elders of our chapel; another was a butcher, another a gas fitter, and a fourth, if I remember rightly, a linen draper. I heard Faraday read & expound often during my childhood, and I remember I liked him best of all the elders...'

AN ANONYMOUS EDITORIAL IN *THE REFEREE*, 21 JUNE 1891

BELOW: *One of the first batteries – a 'Volta's pile' given to Faraday by its inventor, Alessandro Volta. Without the current produced by such batteries, much of Faraday's work would have been impossible.*

Michael received little formal education. At the Sandemanian Sunday school, and at what he called a 'common day-school', he learned basic reading, writing, and arithmetic. Nevertheless, for a boy of his intelligence, this was enough. He also gained a life-long love of learning and books.

Apprentice

When Michael was thirteen, a local bookseller and bookbinder, Mr Riebau, employed him as an errand boy. Riebau soon saw Michael's intelligence and took him on, free of charge, as an apprentice. Surrounded by books all day, Michael read widely. He became fascinated by the wonders of the natural world, which he took as evidence of God's power and glory.

In his mid-teens Michael came across an article on electricity in the *Encyclopaedia Britannica*. The unusual subject immediately fascinated him. In his spare time he began making electrical devices, including his own 'Volta's pile' (see page 8).

AWE-STRUCK

Michael Faraday's apprenticeship lasted seven years. During this time he not only learned all there was to know about books and bookbinding, he also developed into a keen amateur scientist. Robert, his elder brother, helped by paying for him to attend scientific lectures. Faraday also went to meetings of the City Philosophical Society, where like-minded young scientists heard talks, carried out experiments and exchanged ideas.

In 1812, just before Faraday's apprenticeship finished, one of Mr Riebau's customers gave Faraday a ticket to a lecture by Sir Humphry Davy, the famous scientist. Davy was Professor of Chemistry at the Royal Institution, one of Britain's leading establishments for scientific research and teaching. Faraday was awe-struck by the experience. He made notes on what he had heard, added his own illustrations, and bound them up into a book.

ABOVE: *Sir Humphry Davy (1778-1829), the famous scientist and inventor of the miners' safety lamp, who first employed Faraday as a scientist.*

Apprentice no more

In September that year, Faraday left Mr Riebau's and began work as a qualified bookbinder. Although he earned a reasonable wage, he was dissatisfied with his work. He disliked the business side of his trade and was bored by the routine and lack of mental stimulation. What he really wanted was to be a 'natural philosopher' (scientist).

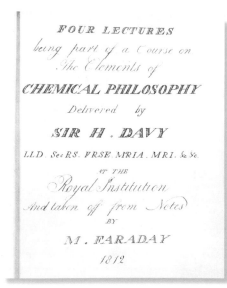

FOUR LECTURES
being part of a Course on
The Elements of
CHEMICAL PHILOSOPHY
Delivered by
SIR H. DAVY
LL.D. Sec.R.S. F.R.S.E. M.R.I.A. M.R.I. &c.
AT THE
Royal Institution
And taken off from Notes
BY
M. FARADAY
1812

LEFT: *The title page of Faraday's notes on Sir Humphrey Davy's lecture at the Royal Institution.*

In vain, Faraday wrote to Sir Joseph Banks, president of the Royal Society. Founded in 1660, in the reign of King Charles II, the Royal Society was Britain's most prestigious scientific organization. Faraday hoped to be offered a post there, but had no luck. In December 1812, he took the bold step of sending the book of notes he had made to Sir Humphry Davy. He accompanied the book with a request for a job – any job – in the scientific world. Although Sir Humphry wrote to say there was no job available, he was clearly impressed with Faraday's work and kept his name in mind.

IN THEIR OWN WORDS

FARADAY'S DISLIKE OF 'TRADE', MEANING BUSINESS, STEMMED FROM HIS SANDEMANIAN BELIEF THAT THE PURSUIT OF WEALTH WAS IMMORAL AND CORRUPTING. THIS IS HOW HE EXPLAINED HIS FIRST APPROACH TO SIR HUMPHRY DAVY:

'My desire to escape from trade, which I thought vicious and selfish, and to enter into the service of Science, which I imagined made its pursuers amiable and liberal, induced me at last to take the bold and simple step of writing to Sir H. Davy expressing my wishes and a hope that, if an opportunity came in his way, he would favour my views.'

RIGHT: *Sir Joseph Banks (1744-1820), the distinguished botanist who turned down Faraday's request for employment at the Royal Society.*

At the Royal Institution

IN FEBRUARY 1813 fortune smiled on Michael Faraday. When a laboratory assistant at the Royal Institution was dismissed for fighting, Sir Humphry Davy remembered the young man who had bound his lecture notes and recommended Michael Faraday as a replacement. Faraday took up his new post on 1 March, earning twenty-five shillings a week with free accommodation in the Royal Institution.

Davy is supposed to have said that Michael Faraday was his greatest discovery. Despite his having only basic mathematics, the new assistant soon became an important part of the professor's research team.

At the end of the year Faraday accompanied the Davys on a grand tour of Europe, visiting many well-known scientists and scientific institutions. Back in London in 1815, Faraday was appointed the Royal Institution's 'Assistant in the Laboratory and Mineral Collection and Superintendent of the Apparatus.' His starting salary of £100 a year was a good salary at the time, but it would remain unchanged until 1853.

BELOW: *The Royal Institution in Albemarle Street, central London, where Faraday spent much of his working life.*

Laying the foundations

Faraday learned and worked incredibly fast. In 1815-16 he helped Davy develop his miner's safety lamp (see panel). The next year he wrote his first research paper, on the limestone of Tuscany. At this time, his main interest was in chemistry, a science much changed by Davy's work. He also came across the idea that substances were held together by forces, or 'bonds', that could be broken. This theory would influence his thinking about electricity.

By 1820 Faraday was a master of laboratory research techniques and knew as much chemistry as anyone alive. He had also proved a popular lecturer at the City Philosophical Society (1815-19). More importantly, he was developing ideas of his own that shortly would amaze the scientific world.

DAVY'S SAFETY LAMP

Before the invention of electric lamps, coal miners carried lamps with naked flames. These often caused fatal explosions by igniting the methane gas found underground. Davy's safety lamp surrounded the lamp's flame with a metal gauze. This allowed air to reach the flame, but absorbed its heat enough to prevent it igniting the surrounding methane.

Metal gauze

Wick

Base

LEFT: *Nothing to fear – Sir Humphry Davy shows miners how to use his safety lamp. A wire gauze prevented the naked flame from igniting explosive methane gas.*

A MAN OF CONTRADICTIONS

Michael Faraday was now thirty and in the prime of life. He was quite short in height, well-built, with large, intelligent eyes and wavy brown hair that he parted in the centre. The upper lip of his broad mouth had a tense look to it. This gave the impression that Faraday sometimes struggled to control himself.

Most people who met Faraday remembered him as good-natured. However, John Tyndall, who knew him very well, thought his personality was more complex. He said Faraday was 'a man of excitable and fiery nature', who, with enormous self-discipline, directed his 'central glow' (main energy) into his work.

Faraday's mental struggles showed themselves in other ways, too. He enjoyed being famous and wanted all his honours listed in his books; yet he disliked being praised in public. (Before his death he insisted that his gravestone should read simply 'Michael Faraday'.) He liked mixing with the rich but was happiest at home. Furthermore, while rejecting scientific research that was not carefully done and exact, he accepted without question that every word of the Bible was true.

IN THEIR OWN WORDS

JOHN TYNDALL, A FUTURE PROFESSOR AT THE ROYAL INSTITUTION, WORKED CLOSELY WITH FARADAY AND UNDERSTOOD HIM AS WELL AS ANYONE. HE ONCE WROTE:

'We have heard much of Faraday's gentleness and sweetness and tenderness. It is all true, but it is very incomplete... Underneath his sweetness and gentleness was the heat of a volcano... Faraday was not slow to anger, but he completely ruled his own spirit...'

RIGHT: *Michael Faraday at about the age of thirty. A calm exterior hid the fiery personality within.*

The pillow of his mind

Wrapped up in his work, Faraday said he had no time for women or marriage. Love, he once declared, was a 'pest and plague'. In 1820, however, he suddenly fell in love with a pretty Sandemanian girl, Sarah Barnard, and pursued her with the same energy as his research.

Happily, Sarah fell in love with him, too, and the couple were married on 12 June 1821. The next month, Faraday was formally admitted to the Sandemanian Church. Although Faraday and Sarah remained childless, their affection for each other never dimmed. Sarah was the much needed voice of normality and calm in Faraday's life. He described her as 'the pillow of my mind'.

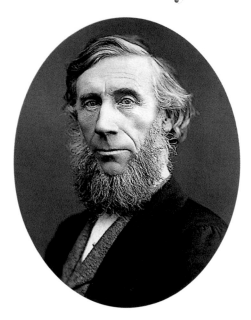

ABOVE: *John Tyndall (1820-93), the self-educated Irish physicist who was both a colleague and friend of Faraday.*

LEFT: *A visit to the laboratory – an imaginative picture of Sarah and Michael Faraday in his laboratory at the Royal Institution. Normally, Faraday worked alone and did not welcome visitors.*

WOLLASTON'S WORRY

While Faraday was courting Sarah Barnard, the scientific world was startled by a paper published by the Danish scientist, Hans Christian Oersted. In 1820, Oersted announced a remarkable discovery: when an electric current flowed through a wire, it produced a magnetic field around that wire.

Oersted's discovery, along with that of the French scientist André-Marie Ampère, who showed that magnetic force was circular, raised an interesting possibility. Perhaps a circular motion could be created using a magnet and an electric

BELOW: *The Danish scientist Hans Christian Oersted (1777-1851) at the moment he noticed the effect an electric current had on a compass needle. This was the first time a link was demonstrated between electricity and magnetism.*

current. Eventually this motion would be harnessed to produce the electric motor.

Davy immediately began researching the idea. After a few false starts, he joined with another scientist, William Wollaston. Wollaston thought a wire with a current going through it could rotate, but he couldn't find a practical way of showing this.

Triumph and shame

Having heard Davy and Wollaston's discussions, in December 1821 Faraday set up his own apparatus to make a wire turn around a magnet (see panel). The experiment worked perfectly. Faraday, a newcomer to the world of electricity, had made the first primitive electric motor.

Eager to publish his results, Faraday went to see Wollaston, who had come up with the revolving wire concept. Unfortunately, Wollaston was away. Faraday foolishly published his results without mentioning Wollaston or Davy.

The publication brought Faraday international recognition. Sadly, it also caused a serious disagreement between himself and Wollaston, who accused him of stealing his ideas. Davy was also annoyed (and probably jealous at Faraday's success). The rift, caused by his own thoughtlessness, upset Faraday deeply. Relations at the Royal Institution did not settle down again until 1823.

RIGHT: *William Wollaston (1766-1828), the successful scientist whom Faraday offended by failing to record his contribution to their joint work.*

FARADAY'S FIRST ELECTRIC MOTOR

Faraday was not interested in the practical applications of his work. Therefore, the apparatus that is sometimes called the 'first electric motor' was not intended as a source of power. It was designed simply to demonstrate electromagnetic rotation. When the current was connected, the magnet in jar 'A' rotated, as did the wire above jar 'B'.

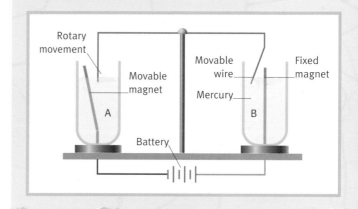

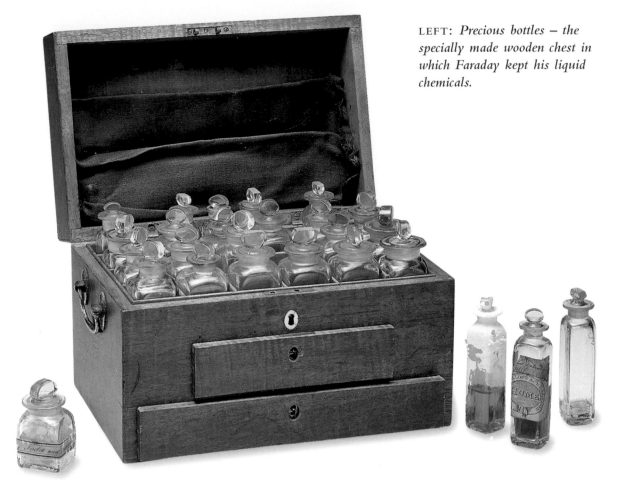

LEFT: *Precious bottles – the specially made wooden chest in which Faraday kept his liquid chemicals.*

BELOW: *An example of Wedgewood pottery. Faraday was employed to analyze the materials used in the production of such items.*

IN DEMAND

By the mid–1820s Michael Faraday was one of Britain's best-known scientists. His discovery of electromagnetic rotation earned him an international reputation, but he was most in demand as a chemist.

Faraday lectured on chemistry to medical students and helped edit the *Quarterly Journal of Science*. Wedgwood potteries, makers of fine china, employed him to analyze their clays. He experimented with the chemistry of metals, too. Working with the instrument maker James Stoddart, he came up with a form of stainless steel. This was one of a number of research projects that brought funds into the Royal Instituton.

Back to chemistry

In 1822, after his brief time with electrical experiments, Faraday returned to chemistry. He had already, in 1820, produced the first known compounds of carbon and chlorine. Now, working in his basement laboratory in the Royal Institution, he continued to experiment with chlorine. The poisonous substance fascinated him and in 1823, acting on a suggestion from Davy, he became the first person to produce the element in liquid form.

Unfortunately, in preparing his report on the liquefaction of chlorine, Faraday again failed to mention Davy's contribution. The angry professor added a paragraph of his own in which he claimed that the experiment had been largely his doing. Once more, a distinct chill settled over the basement of the Royal Institution.

Upset but determined, Faraday pressed on with his work. He liquefied ammonia, carbon dioxide and other gases. These successes led him to suggest that there is a critical temperature above which a gas cannot liquefy. He also mused on the continuity of matter: the fact that solids, liquids and gases can all be converted one to another. And all this he achieved without being able to write a single mathematical equation!

As in all his work, Faraday was not really interested in results for use in industry. He was fascinated by the idea that a substance could be converted from a solid to a liquid and a gas, for instance; but he left it to others to put this to practical use. For example, the oxygen gas fuel for space rockets, is loaded on board in liquid form. Scuba-diving breathing equipment also uses liquid oxygen.

LIQUEFYING CHLORINE

The method Faraday used to liquefy chlorine and other gases was extremely dangerous. The sealed glass tubes often exploded when heated and more than once he suffered temporary eye damage.

BELOW: *Liquid oxygen in action as a Russian rocket is launched. Faraday was one of the first to realize that the same substance could be in gas, liquid or solid form.*

Spreading the Word

BY 1823, MICHAEL FARADAY was so busy outside his laboratory that he had to set aside days when he could work uninterrupted. One of the pressures on his time was acting as an expert witness in the law courts. For such services he was paid handsome fees. Remarkably, he handed all the money over to the Royal Institution to fund further research.

In 1824, Davy persuaded Faraday to become secretary of a new club he had helped found. The Athenaeum, for 'literary and scientific men and followers of the fine arts', held its meetings in the Royal Institution. Faraday found his secretarial tasks got in the way of his scientific work and he resigned after three months. Sir Humphry was not pleased.

BELOW: *London's Athenaeum Club today. Faraday served the club as secretary for three months before leaving to concentrate on his researches.*

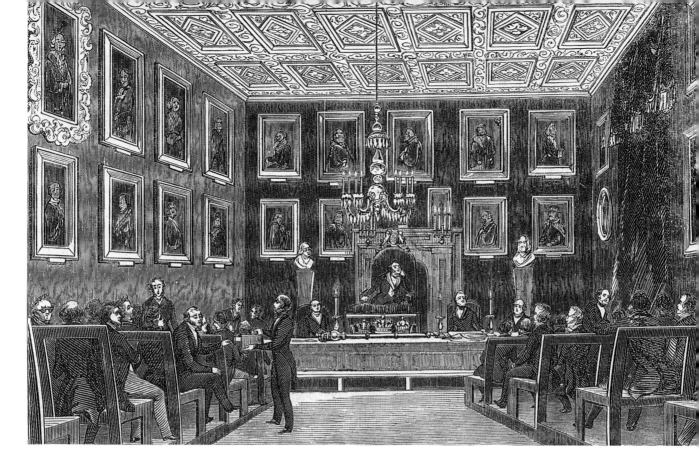

ABOVE: *A meeting of the Royal Society in London in 1843. The walls are adorned with the portraits of famous scientists who had been members of the society since its foundation in 1660.*

The previous year, Faraday had been suggested as a fellow of the Royal Society. Appropriately enough, its president was Sir Humphry Davy. When Faraday was elected a fellow of the Royal Society in 1824, only one member opposed the move: Davy!

Director

Davy was a good-hearted man and his fits of jealousy toward his young protégé never lasted long. In 1825, he suggested that Faraday become Director of the Laboratory at the Royal Institution.

The new position did not bring a higher salary, but it did mean the Faradays could live within the Royal Institution. For Faraday this was ideal – he now had his two great loves, science and Sarah, under the same roof.

IN THEIR OWN WORDS

AFTER DAVY'S DEATH, FARADAY DESCRIBED HOW THE OLDER MAN HAD TRIED TO GET HIM TO TAKE DOWN THE 'CERTIFICATE' THAT ANNOUNCED HIS STANDING FOR ELECTION TO THE ROYAL SOCIETY.

'Sir H. Davy told me I must take down my certificate. I replied... it was put up by my proposers... Then he said, "I as president will take it down..." '

BENZENE AND GLASS

BELOW: *An early nineteenth-century telescope. Faraday spent long hours trying to improve the quality of the optical glass used in such instruments.*

In 1825 Michael Faraday set out to discover what the clear liquid was at the bottom of gas containers delivered to his laboratory. There was a family interest in the research, as his brother Robert worked for the London Gas Company that supplied the gas.

Part of the research involved burning the substance in pure oxygen and accurately measuring the amounts of carbon dioxide and water that this produced. This enabled Faraday to learn the chemical formula of the substance. It was benzene (which he called 'bicarburet of hydrogen'), a vital ingredient of fuels and many products of the modern pharmaceutical industry.

In the same year, Faraday joined a project to improve the quality of glass used in telescopes. The operation was organized by a committee of the Royal Society, chaired by Davy. Faraday found the work very boring. He was saddened by Davy's death in 1829, but it meant that he was free to switch to more interesting projects.

Spreading fame

Although Faraday was not making scientific breakthroughs, his reputation continued to rise. He was already a member of the Paris Academy of Sciences. By 1831 he had been honoured by five more overseas academic societies, including the Imperial Academy of Sciences in St Petersburg, Russia. Before his death, such honours were to multiply ten-fold.

Sarah and Faraday's social life became more glamorous, too. They attended fashionable parties and met some of the great figures of their day, including the painters John Constable and J.M.W. Turner. Later, their circle of acquaintances would expand even wider to include the writer Charles Dickens and the botanist Charles Darwin.

IN THEIR OWN WORDS

MICHAEL AND SARAH LIMITED THE NUMBER OF SOCIAL FUNCTIONS THEY ATTENDED. MICHAEL EXPLAINED POLITELY TO THE FAMOUS ENGINEER SIR JOHN RENNIE THAT HE WENT TO A DINNER PARTY ONLY WHEN IT WAS HOSTED BY A PRESIDENT OF THE ROYAL INSTITUTION:

'Dear Sir,
I am very much obliged to you for your kind invitation but am under necessity declining it because of a general rule which I may not depart from without offending many kind friends – I never dine out except with our Presidents... whose invitations I consider as commands.'

BELOW: *The Institute of France in Paris that houses the Academy of Sciences. This was one of the first overseas institutions to recognize the importance of Faraday's work by making him a member of their institution.*

ABOVE: *The master at work – Faraday lecturing at the Royal Institution. Unusually for a research scientist, he was as brilliant a lecturer as he was a scientist.*

THE TEACHER

Michael Faraday worked only with Sergeant Charles Anderson (see page 4) and never took on any pupils. Surprisingly for such a solitary man, he was enthusiastic about education and was said to be the best scientific lecturer of his day.

At that time a public lecture, with demonstrations, was the best way to spread scientific knowledge to those without a scientific background. It was similar to a modern television documentary programme.

Sir Humphry Davy's brilliant lecturing had inspired Faraday to improve his own public speaking. As a young man he had lectured at the City Philosophical Society, and from 1829 to 1853 he taught chemistry at the Royal Military Academy, Woolwich. However, his most famous teaching work began when he took over as laboratory director at the Royal Institution in 1825.

New lecture courses

Faraday established two courses of lectures to explain complicated subjects in a clear and lively manner. For adults there were evening discourses. These were normally held on Fridays and were open to members of the Royal Institution and their guests. Faraday gave many discourses himself, speaking on topics as varied as electromagnetism, steel nibs for pens, and 'Early Arts: The Bow and Arrow'.

Although childless, Sarah and Faraday loved children. This affection inspired Faraday's Christmas lectures for children. Starting in 1826, the series of six talks over the Christmas period soon became a popular annual event. Faraday delivered nineteen of them himself. The most famous, because it was brilliantly written and interesting, was his 'Chemical History of a Candle', which he gave several times over the years. In another, exciting lecture, to demonstrate the power of electromagnetism he flung heavy pieces of iron household equipment across the room against a huge electromagnet.

IN THEIR OWN WORDS

MUCH OF FARADAY'S SUCCESS AS A LECTURER WAS DUE TO HIS RESPECT FOR THE AUDIENCE. HE REVEALED THIS IN HIS THOUGHTS ON HOW TO LECTURE SUCCESSFULLY:

'[A lecturer's] ...whole behaviour should evince a respect for his audience, and he should in no case forget that he is in their presence... he should never, if possible, turn his back to them.'

Royal Institution of Great Britain,

ALBEMARLE STREET,

December 3, 1827

A

COURSE OF SIX ELEMENTARY LECTURES

ON

CHEMISTRY,

ADAPTED TO A JUVENILE AUDIENCE, WILL BE DELIVERED DURING THE CHRISTMAS RECESS,

BY MICHAEL FARADAY, F.R.S.

Corr. Mem. Royal Acad. Sciences, Paris ; Director of the Laboratory, &c. &c.

The Lectures will commence at Three o'Clock.

Lecture I. Saturday, December 29. Substances generally—Solids, Fluids, Gases—Chemical affinity.

Lecture II. Tuesday, January 1, 1828. Atmospheric Air and its Gases.

Lecture III. Thursday, January 3. Water and its Elements.

Lecture IV. Saturday, January 5. Nitric Acid or Aquafortis—Ammonia or Volatile Alkali—Muriatic Acid or Spirit of Salt—Chlorine, &c.

Lecture V. Tuesday, January 8. Sulphur, Phosphorus, Carbon, and their Acids.

LEFT: *An invitation to wonderland – an advertisement to one of Faraday's children's lectures at the Royal Institution.*

A SENSE OF FUN

Michael Faraday was an obsessive researcher, lecturer and teacher. But his life was not just science. Sarah and he went to the theatre and to concerts. When they could get away, they took holidays in some of the more beautiful and remote parts of Britain and continental Europe.

In the soaring Alps and Devonshire's rolling farmland Faraday saw the same beauty as in the quivering of an electrical wire before a magnet. To him the world and everything in it was a constant reminder of God's miraculous handiwork. 'The book of nature which we have to read,' he once said, 'is written by the finger of God.'

Unlike some deeply religious people at that time, Faraday was not stern and humourless. He was always on good form when his many nephews and nieces came to visit at the Royal Institution. To amuse them he rode a velocipede (an early type of bicycle) round the back of the Institution's lecture theatre. One of his favourite tricks was to drop a piece of potassium into a bowl of water and listen to the children's squeals of delight as it hissed and fizzed over the surface.

ABOVE: *Potassium's spectacular reaction with water, one of Faraday's favourite demonstrations for children.*

BELOW: *A velocipede, an early type of bicycle that Faraday enjoyed riding in and around London.*

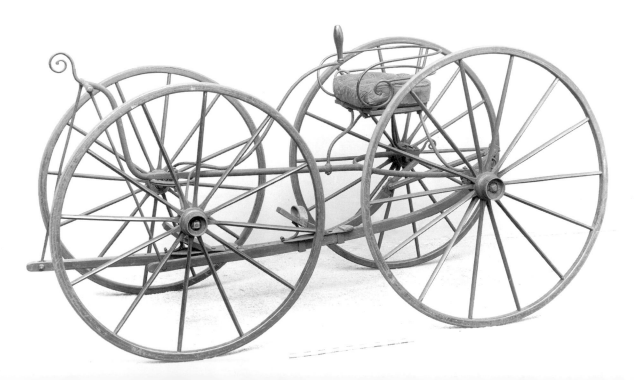

ABOVE: *A haven for a genius – Faraday's study at the Royal Institution. Although never a rich man, Sarah and he lived in reasonable comfort.*

Loyalty

Faraday was a deeply loyal man. In 1827-8 a new university college was being established in London. Faraday was offered the post of Professor of Chemistry.

Although promised new facilities and freedom of research, Faraday rejected the offer. The Royal Institution, he explained, had done so much for him that he could not now desert it. Besides, he had unfinished research to complete. In particular, there were secrets in the properties of electricity that he was determined to unlock.

IN THEIR OWN WORDS

JOHN TYNDALL, WHO WORKED WITH FARADAY AT THE ROYAL INSTITUTION, NOTICED THE LINK BETWEEN RELIGION AND SCIENCE (WHICH TYNDALL CALLS 'PHILOSOPHY') IN FARADAY'S MIND:

'The contemplation of Nature, and his own relation to her, produced in Faraday a kind of spiritual exaltation... His religious feeling and his philosophy could not be kept apart; there was an habitual overflow of the one into the other.'

The Peak of His Powers

OVER CHRISTMAS 1830, Michael Faraday himself delivered the Royal Institution's children's lectures. The subject was one that was once again uppermost in his mind: electricity.

Faraday's particular area of interest was how electricity and magnetism related to each other. Since 1820, when Oersted had discovered that electricity produced a magnetic field (see page 18), Faraday had wondered whether the opposite might be true. Could magnetism somehow produce electricity?

BELOW: *Sir Charles Wheatstone (1802-75), a pioneer in the physics of sound, inventor of the concertina and co-inventor of the electric telegraph.*

Induction

At the time, many scientists believed electricity flowed down a wire like water through a pipe. Faraday thought differently. He saw electricity as moving through a substance (a conductor) by creating tensions in that substance. This was the starting point for his greatest theoretical discovery: electrical induction.

The next stage came in the spring of 1831, when Faraday was working with fellow scientist Sir Charles Wheatstone on the physics of sound. Wheatstone spread powder on a metal plate and vibrated the plate with sound. Faraday was fascinated by the patterns formed in the powder. It gave him the idea that something similar might happen with electricity.

At the end of August 1831, Faraday made his breakthrough. Using two lengths of insulated wire wound round a ring of soft iron, he demonstrated electrical induction (see panel). By the end of the year he had

LEFT: *A coil used by Faraday in induction experiments. It was simply insulated wire wound round a ring of soft metal.*

confirmed his discovery with other experiments. One of the most important involved moving a bar magnet in and out of a coil of wire to produce a current in that wire (see panel). The last and most momentous experiment, as we saw in chapter one, uncovered the principle of the dynamo.

FARADAY DISCOVERS INDUCTION

Both these experiments, carried out in the second half of 1831, demonstrated how a magnetic field could induce an electric current in a wire.

In the top diagram, a current passes through the coiled wire A and magnetizes the iron ring. The magnetized ring induces a current in coiled wire B.

In the bottom diagram, when the bar magnet is moved in and out of the coil (but not when it is held stationary) a current is induced in the coil.

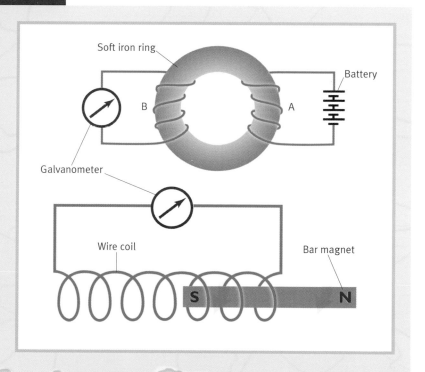

THEORY ONLY

Michael Faraday was still not interested in
pursuing the commercial sides of his
discoveries. This opportunity fell to others. An
American, Joseph Henry, developed electro-
magnets, electric motors and a simple form of
telegraph. A Frenchman (Hippolyte Pixii) and
two Englishmen (Edward Clarke and John
Woolrich) devised more efficient dynamos.

In 1832 Faraday turned his attention to the
four known types of electricity: the new,
induced electricity, 'voltaic' electricity (from a
battery), static electricity and animal electricity
(as in electric eels). Faraday wanted to show
that these were all part of the same
phenomenon. In fact, he discovered a great
deal more.

ABOVE: *Static electricity at its most
spectacular – a lightning storm in
northern Spain. Faraday was one of the
first scientists to distinguish clearly
between the different types of electricity.*

Electrolysis

Scientists knew that when electricity flowed through water,
hydrogen and oxygen were given off. But no one really
understood why electricity had this effect. In 1832-3
Faraday experimented by passing a current through acidic
water. He found that substances built up on the materials
that introduced the electricity into the acidic solution. His
observations on what was going on (see panel) cleared up a
good deal of misunderstanding and utterly changed our
understanding of electro-chemical action, or electrolysis.

As a result of his work, Faraday drew up the First and
Second Laws of Electrochemistry. For many years these were
at the heart of high school and college science courses.
Furthermore, working with the scholar-scientist William
Whewell, he gave us much of the vocabulary still used in
this branch of science: electrolysis, electrode, electrolyte,
anode, cathode and ion.

ELECTROLYSIS

Electrolysis takes place when electricity passes through a liquid or solid known as an electrolyte. The current passes through the electrolyte from one electrode to another. An electrode is a conductor taking the current into and out of the electrolyte. Tiny electrically charged particles from the electrolyte are attracted to one or other electrode.

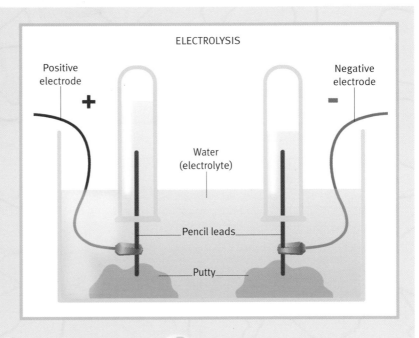

ELECTROLYSIS

Positive electrode

Negative electrode

Water (electrolyte)

Pencil leads

Putty

Today electrochemistry is widely used in industry, for example to produce aluminium, and plate a dull metal with gold or silver. It is remarkable that all this came largely from the researches of a single scientist, working part-time in a basement laboratory.

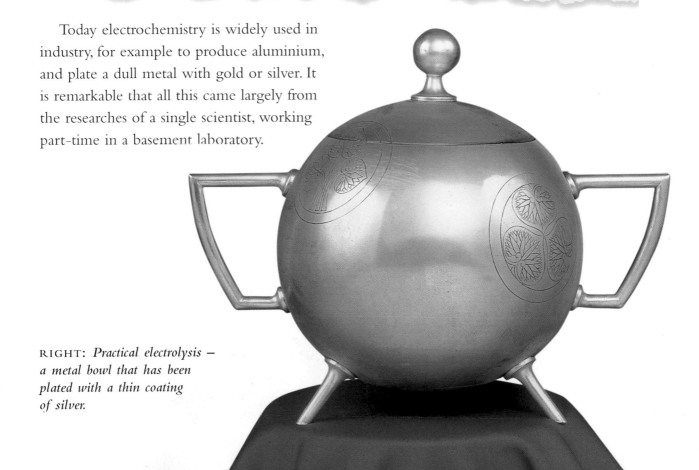

RIGHT: *Practical electrolysis — a metal bowl that has been plated with a thin coating of silver.*

A GOVERNMENT PENSION

After 1831, in order to concentrate on his research, Michael Faraday stopped doing paid consulting work. Although appointed the Royal Institution's first Fullerian Professor of Chemistry in 1834, he was still not well off. Scientists and politicians complained at this treatment of the country's finest scientist. Accordingly, in 1835, as a reward for his achievements the government granted him an annual pension of £300.

The award made no difference to the Faradays' lifestyle. Faraday continued to work flat out. It was not unusual for him to start after breakfast and continue through to eleven o'clock that night.

RIGHT: *An early photograph of Faraday (right) in his laboratory with fellow scientist John Daniell.*

A theory of electricity

From electrolysis Faraday returned to electrical induction. He discovered that all materials – electrical conductors and non-conductors – had an 'inductive capacity'. In other words, they were capable of having electricity induced in them.

By 1839, Faraday had settled his own theory of what electricity was. It was not a sort of invisible fluid, he claimed. Rather, it was a force that acted upon particles within all matter. Through conductors it passed in waves of tension. Non-conductors were more resistant to electricity's waves of tension.

Breakdown

Waves of tension were building up within Faraday, too. For years he had been researching, lecturing, corresponding with leading scientists around the world, and giving advice on such matters as the safety of lighthouses and the state of London's sewers. He had also been becoming more closely involved with the Sandemanian Church.

In 1839, Faraday had some sort of breakdown. He felt dizzy and lost his memory. His doctors advised him to take a complete break.

RIGHT: *Viscount Melbourne (1779-1848), the prime minister whose government granted Faraday a generous state pension in 1835.*

IN THEIR OWN WORDS

WHEN FARADAY FIRST MET THE PRIME MINISTER, LORD MELBOURNE, TO DISCUSS HIS PENSION, THE PRIME MINISTER SAID SOMETHING THAT UPSET THE PROUD SCIENTIST. AS A RESULT, FARADAY WROTE AND TURNED DOWN THE GOVERNMENT'S OFFER:

'My Lord,
The conversation with which your lordship honoured me this afternoon, including as it did, your lordship's opinion of the general character of the pensions given of late to scientific persons, induce me respectfully to decline the favour which I believe your lordship intended for me.'

FORTUNATELY, THE MATTER WAS SOON SORTED OUT AND FARADAY GRATEFULLY ACCEPTED HIS PENSION.

Fading Glory

BELOW: *Burning out – Sarah Faraday with her husband at the time when his great mind was beginning to fail him. Sarah cared for Michael with great devotion until the end of his life.*

MICHAEL FARADAY DID no serious research between 1839 and 1845. We do not know exactly what was wrong with him because medical science was far less advanced than today. His illness may have been physical or mental or a combination of the two.

In 1840, Faraday was made an elder of his Church. This time-consuming position became more difficult when the Church split over interpreting the Bible. Faraday was among several Sandemanians (including members of his family) who were thrown out of the Church. The split did not last long, but for a time it made Faraday deeply depressed.

Recovery

Even so, Faraday was incapable of doing nothing. He still wrote scientific papers and gave lectures. Even when on holiday in Switzerland in 1841, he insisted on walking up to forty miles a day!

By 1845, Faraday was back in his laboratory. At the age of fifty-four, his brain was as active as ever although his memory was fading. He dealt with this by writing down everything important that came into his head.

The force of nature

All his scientific life Faraday had believed in the 'unity of the forces of nature'. By this he meant that there was only one force in the universe, and all lesser forces (such as magnetism, electricity, heat and light) were simply features of the supreme force, God.

Faraday voiced an aspect of this theory in a lecture in 1846 called 'Thoughts on Ray Vibrations'. His suggestion that light and magnetism were somehow related was later proved correct. It was the launching pad for the work of famous scientists such as James Maxwell and Albert Einstein.

ABOVE: *Albert Einstein (1879-1955), perhaps the most famous of the many scientists whose worked rested on foundations laid by Michael Faraday. Faraday's work on light and magnetism was the basis from which Einstein's theory of relativity would emerge.*

ABOVE: *Beyond our dreams – a photograph of distant galaxies, to which we are linked by forces predicted by Faraday.*

LAST RESEARCH

By 1850, Michael Faraday had taken his idea of the unity of the forces of nature a step further. Space, he believed, should not be thought of as a void. He suggested that it was a medium of some sort in which magnetic and electrical forces could make themselves felt. Yet again, he had reached conclusions that would be confirmed and developed by later generations.

Faraday continued to work into the 1850s, although his mind was becoming less sharp now and his memory was steadily growing worse and worse. Sadly, he admitted that he was nervous about starting new research. He was afraid he might repeat someone else's work without realizing it and be accused of copying. Nevertheless, he continued to lecture, and some of his last research on metals and light, presented in 1857, proved remarkably far-sighted. It led the way to a branch of modern chemistry that deals with how substances appear to dissolve together. An example of the practical use of this is the purification of drinking water.

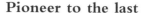

Pioneer to the last

In the same year the Royal Society invited Faraday to become its president. This was the highest honour in British science. Nevertheless, he declined it on health grounds. He was also worried that it might go against the humility demanded by his Sandemanian faith.

On a more practical level, Faraday continued to act as a scientific advisor to various bodies. He could still be found clambering around lighthouses, suggesting improvements to their lights and fog-horns. He also advised the National Gallery in London on how best to preserve ancient paintings. One of his last causes was having science added to the British school curriculum. In this, as in so many fields, he was a bold pioneer.

BELOW: *Nearing the end – Faraday with his family in 1858. Sarah is seated next to him. Seated on the ground are John Tyndall (left) and Jane, the Faradays' niece.*

ABOVE: *A mid-nineteenth century lighthouse. One of Faraday's last projects was examining the possibility of installing electric lights in all lighthouses.*

STRUGGLING ON

By 1860, it was painfully clear that Faraday's mind was failing fast. The Royal Society had decided not to publish the last paper he sent them. In 1861, after a lifetime of loyal service, he retired as a lecturer at the Royal Institution. He still remained in charge of the laboratories, however, and Sarah and he continued to live there.

For four years, increasingly reliant upon his beloved Sarah, Faraday struggled on. Sometimes his thought and speech was quite clear. In his more lucid moments, he investigated the possibility of installing electric lamps in lighthouses. This research led to the eventual conversion of all lighthouses to electricity.

Plain Michael Faraday

In 1864, Faraday stepped down as an elder of his Church. The next year, he resigned from all his other positions, and Sarah and he moved out of the Royal Institution. Queen Victoria, whose husband and elder son had attended Faraday's Christmas lectures in 1855-6, gave the Faradays a house at Hampton Court in London. She offered Faraday a knighthood, too. Not surprisingly, he turned down the offer. He would, he said, prefer to remain plain Michael Faraday.

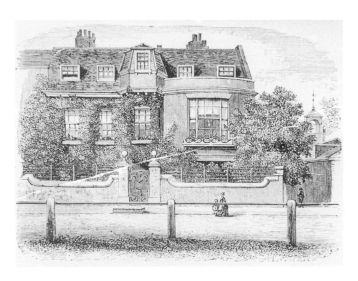

LEFT: *Final home - the house at Hampton Court, London, that Queen Victoria gave to the Faradays.*

Tended by Sarah and his nieces, Faraday spent his last two years in a tragic loneliness. His mind had completely gone. He sat, day after day, staring into space, unable to communicate with anyone.

The greatest scientist of his age finally died on 25 August 1867. At his request he was not buried alongside other famous people in Westminster Abbey. Instead he was laid to rest in a simple grave in London's Highgate Cemetery: honest, plain Michael Faraday to the last.

IN THEIR OWN WORDS

AFTER REJECTING THE OFFER TO BECOME PRESIDENT OF THE ROYAL SOCIETY, FARADAY EXPLAINED TO JOHN TYNDALL WHY HE HAD DONE SO. BY 'INTEGRITY OF... INTELLECT' HE MEANT KEEPING HIS MIND FREE AND INDEPENDENT:

'Tyndall, I must remain plain Michael Faraday to the last; and let me now tell you, that if I accepted the honour which the Royal Society desires to confer upon me, I would not answer for the integrity of my intellect for a single year.'

RIGHT: *Never to be forgotten – the impressive statue of Michael Faraday at the foot of the stairs in the Royal Institution.*

John Tyndall, who succeeded Faraday at the Royal Institution, had no doubt that Faraday's reputation would grow with the passage of time:

'*Taking him for all in all, I think it will be conceded that Michael Faraday was the greatest experimental philosopher the world has ever seen, and I will add the opinion, that the progress of future research will tend, not to dim or to diminish, but to enhance and glorify the labours of this mighty investigator.*'

The Father of Electrical Science

THE PRACTICAL LEGACY of Michael Faraday's work is not immediately obvious. He made no machine or gadget, such as a telephone or light bulb, that we can see working today. Nevertheless, he had as much impact on our world as any scientist of the last 200 years.

The electrical world

Faraday's legacy was one of ideas and theories that others turned to practical use. For example, wherever there is a public supply of electricity, there are motors, generators and

RIGHT: *The city of Hong Kong at night, brilliantly lit by electric lights powered by continuous currents. The means of generating such a current was one of Faraday's most significant discoveries.*

transformers – all devices that stemmed from Faraday's discovery of electrical induction. Indeed, some scientists would argue that our electricity-based world was born in Faraday's laboratory in the basement of the Royal Institution.

Faraday's work in chemistry, magnetism, electrolysis and electromagnetism was almost equally important. His research gave birth to the modern electrochemical industry. This covers all processes that involve chemistry and electricity, such as the manufacture of aluminium and the plating of metals with substances like chrome, tin and silver. He inspired the theory of electromagnetic waves, which in turn led to radio transmission. That all this should be the legacy of one man is almost beyond belief.

ABOVE: *The modern car industry is one of the largest users of the electroplating techniques pioneered by Faraday.*

Generosity, humility, loyalty

The personal side to Faraday's legacy is equally remarkable. For all his fame and undoubted genius, he remained a kindly and humble man, unspoilt by success. He worked not for wealth, but for truth. Throughout his life he remained loyal to his family, his Church and his friends.

Faraday's response to a discovery was a wish to share it with others. This enthusiasm and generosity made him a natural educator. His Christmas lectures, therefore, still going strong more than a century after his death, are a fitting tribute to a truly great scientist and a fine human being.

BELOW: *Still going strong – The Royal Institution's Christmas lectures for children, begun by Faraday, are as popular as ever. Here a recent lecturer, neuroscientist Professor Susan Greenfield, is talking with her students during a lecture.*

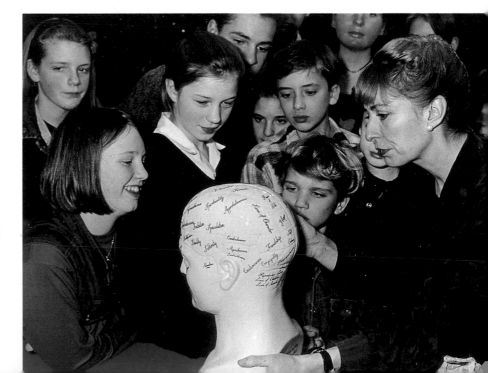

Timeline

c.1730

John Glas founds the sect that becomes the Sandemanians.

1778

Sir Joseph Banks becomes president of the Royal Society.

1791

James and Margaret Faraday move to London from Yorkshire.
22 SEPTEMBER: Michael Faraday born.

1800

Alessandro Volta makes the first electric battery.

1802

Margaret Faraday, Michael's favourite sister, born.

1805

Faraday is apprenticed to a bookbinder, Mr Riebau.

1812

Faraday attends a scientific lecture given by Sir Humphry Davy. He decides he wants to be a scientist. His apprenticeship ends and he writes to Sir Joseph Banks and Davy asking for employment.

1813

Faraday is employed as a laboratory assistant at the Royal Institution.
Leaves for a tour of continental Europe with Sir Humphry and Lady Davy (until 1815).

1815

Faraday begins lecturing at the City Philosophical Society, London.

1815–16

Faraday works with Davy on his miners' safety lamp.

1816

Faraday publishes his first research paper.

1818–24

Faraday doing important research into the properties of steel alloys.

1820

Oersted discovers the magnetic field around an electric wire.
Faraday makes the first compounds of chlorine and carbon.

1821

12 JUNE: Faraday marries Sarah Barnard.
SEPTEMBER: Faraday makes the first electric motor.

1823

Faraday produces liquid chlorine.

1824

The Royal Society invites Faraday to become a fellow.

1825

Faraday appointed Director of the Laboratory at the Royal Institution. He establishes his evening discourses and Christmas lectures for children.

1825–29

Faraday working to improve the quality of lenses (used in telescopes, for example).

1826

Christmas lectures at the Royal Institution begin.

1829

Faraday begins teaching chemistry at the Royal Military Academy, Woolwich (to 1853).

1831

Faraday discovers electro-magnetic induction and makes the first dynamo.
Also working on the patterns of vibrations made by sound.

1832

Faraday confirms the unity of all types of electricity.

1833

Faraday writes the first Two Laws of Electrochemistry.

1834

Faraday becomes the Royal Institution's first Fullerian Professor of Chemistry.

1835

Faraday receives a government pension. Faraday researching how electricity passes through gasses.

1836

Faraday becomes scientific advisor to Trinity House, the body that oversees lighthouses and pilots around the coast of Britain.

1838

Wheatstone invents the stereoscope, a device that enables an image to appear solid.

1839

Faraday produces his theory of electricity, he falls ill and is unable to do further serious research until 1845.

1840

Faraday becomes an elder of the Sandemanian Church.

1841

Faraday and Sarah holiday in Switzerland.

1845–50

Faraday researching the relationship between electricity, light and magnetism.

1846

Faraday delivers his famous lecture, 'Thoughts on Ray Vibrations'.

1849

Faraday researching the relationship between electricity and gravity.

1853

John Tyndall becomes a lecturer at the Royal Institution.

1857

Faraday publishes research into light and metals. He refuses the presidency of the Royal Society. Also working on the relationship between time and magnetism.

1860

Faraday delivers his most famous series of Christmas lectures, 'The Chemical History of a Candle'.

1861

Faraday resigns as lecturer at the Royal Institution.

1864

Faraday resigns from all his posts.

1865

Faraday and Sarah retire to a house at Hampton Court.

1867

25 AUGUST: Michael Faraday dies, aged 75.

1922

Institution of Electrical Engineers establish a Faraday Medal for notable achievement in the field of electrical engineering.

1923

Institution of Electrical Engineers establish the Faraday Lectures.

Glossary

Apprentice
Someone working with a qualified employer to learn a craft or trade.

Botanist
Expert in plant life.

Chlorine
Greeny-yellow element that is a gas at normal temperature and pressure.

Compound
Substance made up of two or more elements.

Conductor
Substance through which electricity passes easily.

Congregation
The worshippers at a church or other religious meeting place.

Critical temperature
The temperature at which a change takes place in a substance, such as boiling or freezing.

Discourse
Discussion or lecture.

Dynamo
Machine that converts mechanical energy into electrical energy.

Elder
Senior member of a congregation.

Electrical induction
Creation of an electric current by movement in a magnetic field.

Electrochemistry
Science relating chemistry and electricity.

Electrode
Point at which an electric current moves from one medium to another. There is an electrode on either end of a battery (cell) for example.

Electrolysis
Using electricity to break down a compound into its elements.

Electromagnetism
Relationship between electricity and magnetism.

Element
Substance made up of one type of atom.

Fellow
Invited member of an exclusive club or group, such as the Royal Society.

Galvanometer
Instrument for measuring electric currents.

Generator
See dynamo.

Liquefaction
Making a substance liquid.

Magnetic field
Area around a magnet in which its magnetism operates.

Methane
Gas made up of hydrogen and carbon.

Muriate
Old-fashioned term meaning containing chlorine.

Neuroscientist
A scientist who studies the nervous system.

Pharmaceutical
Relating to the industry that makes medicines.

Pole
One end of a magnet, described as either 'north' or 'south'.

Potassium
A reactive element.

Protégé
Someone who is guided and looked after by a more experienced person.

Rigorous
Strict and exact.

Royal Institution
British organization of scientific research and teaching founded in 1799. Its headquarters are in London.

Royal Society
Britain's leading scientific society, founded in 1660.

Sandemanians
Christian Protestant Church founded in Scotland in about 1730.

Telegraph
Device for sending coded messages down a wire.

Theory of relativity
The principle that it makes no sense to state that an object moves, except in relation to another object.

Transformer
Device for changing the strength or form of an electric current.

Void
Totally empty space.